Through Blessed-Tinted Glasses

A Devotional Journey

Josie Holston Glenn

WestBow Press books may be ordered through booksellers or by contacting:

WestBow Press
A Division of Thomas Nelson & Zondervan
1663 Liberty Drive
Bloomington, IN 47403
www.westbowpress.com
844-714-3454

ISBN: 978-1-6642-4269-2 (sc)
ISBN: 978-1-6642-4268-5 (e)

Print information available on the last page.

WestBow Press rev. date: 08/25/2021

"COMMIT TO THE LORD WHATEVER YOU DO
AND HE WILL ESTABLISH YOUR PLANS"

PROVERBS 16:3 (NIV)

Contents

Acknowledgements

This book is dedicated to all of those incredible people who crossed my paths too many times to individually thank on this ackowledgement page. However, spiritual thanks to Pastor Leon McDaniels, Sr Paradise Baptist Church Oakland, CA who became my spiritual father helping to give life to an important aspect of my life that has fueled much of what i've learned through his awesome leadership and guidance through his sensitivity to the Holy Spirit and his obedience to God.

Special thanks to Mr. Calvin Rubin, my high school instructor who taught me typing skills along with mentoring me for lifelong skills in fitting into the job market; my son, Chucky for his financial support; to Deja, my granddaughter, thanks for "driving Ms. Josie"; my wonderful sisters (Tina, Betty, Shirley) and Joe Jr. my famous artist brother for spiritual and moral support; Cherie Saunders, my beautiful niece with jouralistic support; and Thembe Fulse and Evette Carpenter for IT Assistance. And so to you all "thanks"

Dedication

This book is dedicated to my mother - Viola Holston — the incredible "saint" who died June 28, 1996.

Thanks my dear mother for providing me a well-balanced, happy home life through my growing up years. You lit the flames within me to understand that whoever was spared personal pain must feel compelled to share in helping to alleviate the misery which surrounds us.

This book has been in the making for many years as God has continually spoken to me to encourage others to also look at their lives through blessed-tinted glasses.

Every life, like every journey, has a story. The spiritual journey as told by Siri Aurobindo is "continually falling on your face, getting up, brushing yourself off while looking sheepishly at God while taking another step."

My story - not me the storyteller — is important because it's all about continuing to thank God for every opportunity He has given to me to continuously seek His wisdom.

The Testimony

MOTHER GOT OFF the Greyhound bus - her beautiful dark eyes sparkling, her hickory nut colored cheeks moist and shining. She declared - "Praise the Lord, I'm completely healed! Look at me, Joseline. Don't you see how healthy I look! Oh, the amazing power of having faith in God to heal my body! I'm so excited and I can't wait to get home and show my miracle."

Her first attack of kidney trouble came in early 1956. The pain was so intense that she was hospitalized for two weeks although she prayed for God to heal her body. Those prayers seemed to go unanswered. "it wasn't God's perfect time yet," she later explained.

November 1957, she was again rushed to the hospital for over a month. The doctors performed surgery, but unsuccessfully. Her left kidney had deteriorated. "Your diseased kidney needs to be removed" the doctor gently advised. "It is killing you."

My mother kept on praying while spending quality time alone with the Lord Her Savior. She repeated her favorite scriptures over and over - "I can do all things through Christ who strengthens me - Philippians 4:13 and Be careful for nothing but in everything by prayer and supplication with thanksgiving let your requests be made known unto God... (Philippians 4:6)" My baby brother, Donny, reminded me in a telephone call from Florida on Super Bowl Sunday - 2013 that I had "omitted a major part to our mother's Testimony." He reminded me that she not only asked the Lord to heal her but she specifically asked that He keep her alive until her baby (Donny) was 15 years old!" Needless to say that at the time of her miraculous healing, Donny was eleven years old. She lived way past her request to God - Donny was actually 49 years old when she died. God gave her 34 extraordinary more years past her request concerning Donny's age.

after several uneventful months, mother called me into the room and said "Joseline, Mrs. Kleinpeter asked me if I knew anyone who would be willing to drive her station wagon down to Key Biscayne, Florida to her summer home — all expenses to be totally covered?"

I told her "I can do it." She explained that was where the Oral Roberts Miracle Healing Crusade was going to take place. "Will you be able to get off from your job and go with me?" she asked.

Me? One of the six kids (number two from the top). Shirley Jean, the oldest has already gone off to Maryland

State College and I've just started my good government job (Clerk-Typist, GS-3 - take home pay $99 every two weeks). "Yes, mother" I said. "I'll ask my boss if she will grant me annual leave.

So, my mother and I set off for Florida from our modest home in Chevy Chase, Maryland even though she had no money and I had a little cash. But miraculously, God provided all we needed. Remember Mrs. Kleinpeter - the wealthy employer of mother? Mother worked for her (cleaning and cooking her meals) for many years. It was Mrs. Kleinpeter's habit to spend the summer months in her Florida home. Of course, she would need her station wagon. So, she provided all the money we needed for gas, food and other "incidentals."

Our "Triptik" was prepared by AAA — our bags loaded in the station wagon, goodbyes said and on a sunny morning in January 1958 we began our journey heading for Key Biscayne, Florida.

Joseline, she said "just trust the Lord that we will reach our destination safely. Don't worry, God will take care of us."

Mother was still sick although I didn't realize how sick at the time. She slept and prayed most of the way even though she was able to drive a little bit. We drove from dawn to dusk spending three nights in South Carolina, Georgia and Tennessee. Remember the laws that prohibited Black people from acquiring rooms in motels? How fortunate that God provided incredible, kind Black people (three times in three states) to put us up for the night in their homes.

Our ride down through the racist south was without incident. We sang praise songs such as "if it hadn't been for the Lord on my side, where would I be..."

Just as we drove into Florida heading for the causeway that led to the island of Key Biscayne, mother said "let's drive around a bit and see what's here." Lo and behold! In plain full view was the Oral Roberts Tent Meeting!

Ok, "let's drive on to the Kleinpeter home. I'm alright now."

"Well, Joseline here we are just you, me and God. Let's get a good night's sleep. Let's pray for those nice people who took us in."

It was dusk dark as we pulled into the Kleinpeter driveway. After opening the door and looking around at all the beautiful furniture covered with white sheets, we found the refrigerator fully stocked, heater working and all was well. My seventeen year old brain was "blown away" by the beautiful home we stayed in.

Just as we were preparing for bed, mother dropped this little bomb on me! "now Joseline, tomorrow morning, I'll be taking you over to the Greyhound bus station for your return trip home. I'm going to be fine. Remember I'm trusting in the Lord and not leaning to my own understanding.... (Proverbs 3:5-6 NIV)

"I need to be all alone with God. I'll call you all when He is finished with me."

The testimony: God healed my mother's body, mind and spirit. Further x-rays proved the replacement of the diseased kidney with a brand new healthy one. She was subsequently discharged from the hospital and written up in their medical records at George Washington Hospital in Washington, D.C. as a "miracle" patient. Nothing else could adequately describe the divine intervention from God.

Excerpt from NIV Luke 17:11-19 "one of them, when he saw he was healed, came back praising God in a loud voice...threw himself at Jesus' feet and thanked him....Jesus asked, were not all 10 cleansed?..."has no one returned to give praise to God..."

From that moment of healing to her death in 1996 at the age of 80, mother never had any problems with her kidneys. "I'm a new creature" she often stated. Following her healing, every single year she told her story at a testimonial service at Lee's A.M.E. Church in Kensington, Maryland on the third Sunday in January.

Mother died on June 28, 1996 after testifying one more time (38th time) in January 1996!

38th

HOLSTON TESTIMONIAL SERVICE

Sunday, the twenty-eighth of January
Nineteen Hundred and Ninety six

"I'm living proof that not only does the Lord save our souls, but he can also heal our bodies if we simply believe! That's the Good News of the Christ I serve." (mother's quote)

I know this is a true story for I lived it right alongside my precious mother - Viola Holston.

Out of the Whirlwind Surviving "Confused Cells" (Cancer) Treatment

I FACED AND survived the dreaded diagnosis of breast cancer. My ability to laugh through my troubles helped sustain me every step of the way. I purposely looked for humorous situations that helped alter my perceptions. I reflected on the fact that we are God's only creatures who have the ability to laugh and rejoice through laughter for being alive. Laughter flings open the shutters and lets the sunshine in. A shared gift of laughter is really a priceless gift for our spirits. And it became a great poke in the eye to the adversary "confused cells" (cancer) that I was suddenly facing.

Chemotherapy became my "Kemo Shark!" - my hero, fearless and tireless in its fight against my "confused cells" (a name I gave to cancer). Kemo Shark was a strong warrior who found and killed confused cells but had many side effects too. His vision was not perfect so he sometimes killed healthy cells. He did not know the difference between hair, fingernails or stomach cells. All fast growing cells took a beating. Thank goodness they didn't die but just took time to get well. So, I lost all my hair, my head got sensitive and my scalp hurt. My stomach felt queasy while ingesting Kemo Shark through my blood stream.

I cannot pinpoint the exact moment when humor became a purposeful part of my treatment. I remember the "aha" moment that altered my thinking profoundly. It was at the Cat Scan office where I was given a large container of liquid to drink prior to receiving the test. I happened to look across the room and there sat an at least 250 pound lady drinking the same amount of liquid given to me. I began to laugh until tears fell and I had to go to the bathroom to contain my tears and laughter. Since I had only consumed 1/3 of the mixture, I asked the technician who smiled and said "okay, that's enough.

I'm so glad that I had the fortitude to focus on healing rather than being afraid. I may have had "confused cells" but I got to choose my reaction which was to avoid the morbid approach so popular in the media. Things connecting one thing to another are called bridges. Friends (thanks Ludie) and family were my greatest bridges but I found out that some of my path needed to be travelled alone — with just me and God. All these difficulties fighting with "confused cells" was just a fork in my road. I got to choose which track to take. Either breakdown or breakthrough. With the help of God, I chose BREAKTHROUGH! Fall 2005 - Fall 2012 - fighting "confused cells"

Am I really cured? I will always be on the alert, watching earnestly for any returning symptions. I continue to celebrate with others who beat the odds (that's the group I've chosen to be in). Nevertheless, God is in control and always will be, no matter what crosses my path. Every day that I am here, I'll live my life as if it were my last day. I thank God that each day that passes that God's glory shines on me. I thank God for my healing and I trust Him to continue to keep me since His promises are like a warm security blanket that wraps itself all around me.

Growing Up Black in Chevy Chase, Maryland

LAWS IN AMERICA stopped me from using certain public water fountains, restrooms, restaurants (no sitting down at counters reserved for the "whites")

Looking back, I was blessed to be a member of an intact, loving family complete with mother, daddy, sisters (Shirley, Betty, Tina) and brothers (Joe and Donny). We lived joyously together through troubles of poverty (I was grown before I actually knew we lived "below the poverty line)! Laughter and fun always permeated our lives day after glorious day.

The day I was born on mother and daddy's 8th wedding anniversary, I became the special "kid" named Joseline - after Joseph my father. There's a story included in the book written from my father's voice called "we named her Joseline."

Living in Chevy Chase, Maryland meant walking to the "lake" where white folks would be swimming in their lone pool splashing and laughing and having a royal good time. Of course, because of the "law" we just stood outside and watched enviously while never really understanding why we were not allowed to join in the fun. So, we grouped together and created our own enjoyment including digging a big hole in our backyard and filling it up with water. Of course, it turned into quite a mud mess!

Our street - Hawkins Lane is smack dab behind the Naval Medical Center and across from the famous Chevy Chase Golf Club where all 15 homes contained Black residents. We also lived within walking distance to all white Bethesda Chevy Chase High School. We of course (because of the "law") were "bussed" 18 miles roundtrip to segregated schools in Rockville, Maryland (segregated 1927-1960). However, riding the bus was one of the highlights of our days — we had so much fun, laughter and companionship and love amongst the busload of beautiful Black kids supervised with love by Mr. Jim, our caring bus driver. He always had all kinds of treats to give us. You could call him one of our "extended" relatives who watched over us all.

I entered first grade September 19, 1944. In addition to the schools we attended, there were Black families throughout Montgomery County who also rode school buses to reach the same segregated schools.

Rockville Elementary School was all Black - teachers, principal and staff. September 1951, my education continued at Lincoln Junior High School in Rockville, Maryland. Lots of new experiences such as going to different rooms for each class and taking physical education. One hundred thirty (130) of us graduated bound for Carver High School the following September.

As with Lincoln Junior High, Carver (George Washington Carver) continued to serve the Black populaton of Montgomery County. For three years, Carver offered educational opportunities in the academic, commercial, general and vocational curricula. Our instructors made sure that we were prepared to compete with the "outside white" world.

Integration reared its ugly head in my 12th year of segregated education. Those in "charge" met and decided that Black and white kids should go to school together. Let me set the stage: Here I am - an A student with a GPA of 4.0 and prepared to slide my way through 12th grade on my academic reputation alone. And along comes (unwanted) integration!

Since all this was brand new, my father came to me and gave me the option of going to the white school in our neighborhood or did I want to continue at the Black school still able to ride the coveted school bus. Clearly, there was only one answer — to stay put at Carver High School. So, I was not required to "integrate." A different decision was required for my younger siblings who were not so lucky. My sisters Betty (one year behind me) and Tina (two years behind me) under much duress had to go and that's another story all together.

Fifty-six of us (all Black) graduated June 13, 1956. I was immediately recruited by the federal government to work for the Women's Bureau of the Labor Department. It was here that my integrated living got a real workout. Because I lived a very sheltered segregated existence for all those years, I had no idea how cruel and uncaring people could be simply because of the color of my skin. How I stayed optimistic and peaceful had to be my blessed-tinted glasses and my parents who had insulated me with the loving condition of my home and school and neighborhood - all who looked just like me.

Hawkins Lane - A Lane with Legacy

HAWKINS LANE LOOKS like a quiet country lane surrounded by dense woods. A narrow, easily missed dead-end street off Jones Bridge Road between Connecticut Avenue and Rockville Pike. It's boardered by Bethesda Naval Hospital smack in the middle of the bustling Washington, D.C. suburbs.

Hawkins Lane - a legacy of James H. Hawkins born into slavery who acquired three acres from descendants of his white namesake. (slave owners gave their slaves their names). His son, Sam Hawkins built the road and several houses for family members. He sold a few lots for development to Russell Mizell whose family owned the lumber yard and hardware store in Kesington, Maryland,

Hawkins Lane used to be a thriving Black community in North Chevy Chase - 12 houses actually on the Lane and two more that adjoined on Jones Bridge Road. There was no door to door mail delivery. Where the Lane meets the main road (Jones Bridge Road) a dozen mailboxes stood like sentries.

It was in the late fifties. I was sitting at our (me and Shirley's) bedroom window at 11 Hawkins Lane where I gazed out beyond the maple trees, over the grass through the hedges to the woods in the back of the house. Hawkins Lane a noble street, narrow and stretching for less than one-quarter of a mile, unpaved and deadended down by the DeGraffe's house at the very end of the lane. Totally bordering entire Hawkins Lane was a chain-link fence surrounding Naval Medical Center (yes, Bethesda Naval Medical Center where all injured or ill United States Presidents received medical attention.

It was late summer and there had been good rain all that year. Rain was important since good rains meant productive gardens with large, ripened apples, grapes, plums, tomatoes, black walnuts, green beans, cherries and so forth and so on. Our house had its own garden in the back but our produce paled compared to Mr. Stewart's garden right next door and Mr. Sam Hawkins' garden down at the end of the Lane (Hawkins Lane - named after Mr. Hawkins). The yellow flesh of a summer squash from either of these two gardens —boiled then softened with a lump of real butter was one of God's greatest gifts to us. And they tasted so good too with a slice of vine-ripened tomatoes still warm from the sun.

Mr. Hawkins forbidded us kids from roaming through his massive garden and, on many occasions, we found ourselves running "for our lives" to get away from him. Mr. Stewart couldn't care less how much we gathered from his garden. Marie (one of my best friends) spent many hours playing in the garden and helping ourselves to his fine produce.

On that day while sitting at the window, I allowed my thoughts to wander. There was nothing in particular to do. School was out and there were no outstanding matters needing investigation. All was quiet on Hawkins Lane. It was too early for mother and daddy to come home and the brothers and sisters were either reading, playing marbles, pick-up sticks or jacks. The brothers (Joe and Donny) were busy building their soap box car for the upcoming Soap Box Derby. There were so many good things about the "good" old days and it kind of made me sad to think that some of these ways had to die. But not this day so I kept on day dreaming the day away.

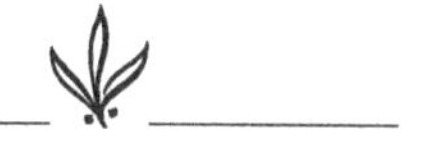

We Named Her "Joseline" (Story Told in Father's Voice)

LET ME BEGIN by saying that I like kids. Nothing I've ever done has given me more joy and reward than being the father of my six kids. Knitted in between these joys and rewards was the natural strife of family life — the little tensions and conflicts that come from trying to create civilized grownups out of kids while struggling to feed and clothe them. Viola (I call her BeBe) used me as her authority figure to discipline and teach these kids the ways of the outside world — kind of what it's actually like being Black in the very white community that surrounded our Black community. My job is to go to work — to be the breadwinner, the provider. Whenever the kids acted up I was characterized as the heavyweight disciplinarian. "Wait til your father gets home, you're really going to get it." Although the threatened "whippings" rarely happened seemed as though her threat alone seemed to keep everybody in check. Back in those days, parents had total authority to dish out any discipline deemed necessary. These kids got away with lots of things with their mother but everyone of them feared what would happen when I got home.

Going back to April 18, 1932, I married by beautiful wife and pretty soon the kids started coming. First, there were two mishaps where our first two baby girls died — one in childbirth and the second one shortly after birth. Then we had Shirley Jean born in 1937. She became a sort of princess for all of one and a half years. Little did she know that her lonely existence as "only kid" was about to drastically change.

On April 18, 1939 our second baby girl was born. This one started out pretty special since her day of birth was our eighth wedding anniversary. Looked like we probably would not have any more kids so we decided to name her after me - Joseph. So her name - Joseline - sort of a junior to me.

April became a big month for celebrations in our family. My birthday - April 1st; our wedding anniversary April 18th and to top it off Joseline born on April 18th which was our 8th wedding anniversary. Consequently, Joseline became my "special" baby girl. Of course, we thought that was it — two beautiful daughters but low and behold! Within the next five years, we produced Betty Lee, Ruth Marie (Tina), Joseph Jr. - we could have waited for the junior but it was too late) and baby Samuel Donald. What a way to go Joe, said everybody!

My Joseline continued to be my favorite (don't tell the rest of them) throughout my life.

Snow Days

IT'S 3:30 A.M. All is quiet in and outside. The whole family is sound asleep except me. I lay quietly in my bed next to my sister (Shirley Jean) who is sound asleep in her bed. I'm listening to the total quietness that awakened me. The birds are not up yet. No cars zooming to and fro. The silence is like a warm blanket covering me completely. All is still and silent. There are no walking footsteps crunching through the gravel. No radios or TVs blaring mindless tunes or chattering reporters harping on and on about the "troubles" of the world. Just extraordinary silence as I listened to my breath going in and out - confirming my aliveness. Every ordinary noise completely muted. I drift back to sleep and enjoy the comfort of quietness.

It's time to get up! I leap out of bed as the following radio broadcast blasts out: "Montgomery County schools are closed today because of the snow covering the ground - up to 12 inches in most areas." Yippee!!! No school for us today. What a wonderful gift! We get to play outside until we are too cold and our fingers and toes feel frozen. Flying down the hill on our homemade sleds (actually cardboard boxes turned sideways) had to be the best treat to an eleven year old kid without a care in the world — all credited to the wonderful exquisite snow that fell silently throughout the night!

Disconnected - With No Particular Order

IS THERE A way to avoid loud talking people on their "smart" phones? How about the texting and walking group that walks right into you without even looking up?

you are wasting your time if you are holding anyone else accountable for your happiness.

I must keep moving full speed ahead! I must concentrate on treating this life as what it really is — a gift from God. Each day, I vow to start my day by thanking God for creating unique - one of a kind — me. I promise to try to make it all worthwhile.

Ever got lost in a mall's parking lot? Yep, happened to me. Took me one-half hour to find my car. Frustrating experience.

Today, I laughed out loud over a very humorous situation which I was involved in. I'm trying not to take my life too seriously. Just going to concentrate on showing kindness. An anonymous person said that if you can't change your circumstances, change your perspective! Hmm.

Are You Tenderheaded?

(TENDERHEADED) A CONDITION in which the scalp is very sensitive to the combing, tugging and pulling of the hair characteristic in Black hair care often accompanied by tears. Our hair speaks with a voice as soft as cotton. If you listen closely —put your ear right up to it and listen to its secrets. Like the soothing peace it knew before being yanked out of Africa. Like the neglect it endured sweating under rags in the sun-lashed fields of the South. And, even today, it speaks of its restless quest for home —a place that must be somewhere between Africa and America. Between being rambunctious and restrained, between personally and socially "acceptable."

In the 1960s, while I was still a young mother, the civil rights movement was evolving and a resurgent interest in things connected with Black History came to the forefront. So, many of us were transforming our hair from "permanent waves" using harsh chemicals to get hair straight to just being "natural." Suddenly, with the new awareness of pride in being Black, we dared to see ourselves as beautiful Black women and men. The "natural - Afro" era heightened my already good self-esteem which also caused me to visibly assimilate myself into a society that seemed to only value caucasian beauty - blond, straight hair and pink skin. So, I wore them all: braids, cornrows, locks and twists — so glad to adopt the healthier grooming regimen necessary for healthy hair and scalp.

Hair, even today, is still a very emotional, even political issue, loaded with centuries of complicated psychological and sociological kinks and tangles sometimes volatile enough to provoke a fight, a lawsuit or feelings of shame. Too many people still talk about "good" and "bad"* hair. Women have gotten fired from jobs while being ostracized because they chose to let their African roots push through.

*(bad hair - tightly coiled, coarse hair that is thought to be hard to manage and generally short. Also known as "nappy", tight hair or "mailman hair as in "every knot got its own route!"

Hair has always been a subject fraught with trouble. Just try to imagine enduring the hot-comb treatment. A metal, heavy comb heated on the stove until it became smoking hot, then placed right up next to your scalp to loosen and straighten your course hair. That heavy metal tool used to have the power to make you feel pretty or, when accidently touched to your skin pain was actually inflicted and became a burn.

By the time I reached the first grade, we all realized that our hair texture actually added to or diminished our social status. It took many, many years to erase those negative misconceptions.

Approximately 70 percent of Black women still wear straightened hair, still hoping somehow they will be accepted and "be like them."

Without a doubt, women like media mogul Oprah Winfrey and Congresswoman Maxine Waters have perfected their impeccably coiffed hair that aided them in cracking through a series of glass ceilings leading straight to the top!

Wise Sayings

DON'T EVER STUMBLE over something behind you.

Faith to me is like WiFi: its invisible but it has power to connect you to what you need. (NIV Proverbs 16:3)

Angela Bassett said "don't settle for average. Bring your best to the moment. Then, whether it fails or succeeds, at least you know you gave it all you have."

Today, I'm noticing Happy Things! I cherish this very moment. Enjoying a good cup of coffee, taking a nap and at peace.

Laughter is really good therapy. It's the best medicine and easy to administer, costs nothing and has no unplesant side-effects. Sebastien-Roch said that the most wasted day is that in which we have not laughed. (God must have had a good laugh when he made feet!)

Laughter is good for you! If stressed out, angry or sad - laugh. It can be physically and emotionally therapeutic.

When you laugh, you discharge tension associated with at least four primary negative emotions - depression, anxiety, fear and anger. Any of these can lead to diseases that shorten your life. So, laugh.

If you are patient in one moment of anger you will save a thousand days of sorrow (Chinese Proverb)

When life gives you lemons, throw them back and pray for chocolate!

That the birds of worry and care fly above your head, this you cannot change but that they build nests in your hair — this you can prevent! (Chinese Proverb)

Make an effort to be thankful for who you are and what you have each day.

Take off your spiritual police badge and stop trying to fix others.

Follow the Lord! “He that follows me, walks not in darkness (NIV John 8:12)

Fill your world with color and beauty.

A smile engages 42 muscles which helps lower brain temperature.

It’s up to each of us to stand guard at the portals of our minds to watch our every thought.

Kindness is the rent we must pay for the space we occupy on this planet.

I choose to view my world through blessed-tinted glasses!

The man who removes a mountain begins by carrying away small stones (Chinese Proverb)

Life is an immense journey and each of us has only one lifetime to travel it.

Carry your own weather.

Robert Kennedy said that "20 percent of the people are against everything all the time."

Practice being healthy and happy.

Dr. Dale Anderson said "it's no mystery that we become healthy by acting like healthy people."

Study God's Word. Pray without ceasing. Let the Holy Spirit lead to joyful obedience to God. Results: Mind changed; will changed and we become new born babies (Viola Holston)

Let go and let God (Viola Holston)

Don't look now but your influence is showing — in the entries you are writing each day in the gospel according to you! You are writing each day a letter to others. Take care that the writing is true. Tis may be the only gospel that some person will read - that gospel according to you!

So live then that men may seek your autograph and not your fingerprints! (Viola Holston)

Hands are one of God's niftiest ideas

Defeat isn't bitter if you don't swallow it.

Call on God for help, but row away from the rocks.

Other names for failure: wait, too busy, good enough, not my job, tomorrow.

Of all the things you wear, your expression is the most important.

Dr. Steven Hawking said "we live on a minor planet of a very average star located within the outer limits of one of a hundred thousand million galaxies. How is that for a shift in perspective? Given this information, are your troubles and cares really that big?"

Life is not a stress rehearsal.

Stay happy! live well, love much. Believe in yourself and laugh often.

Never mix yourself up uninvited in other people's business.

We had no childproof lids on medicine bottles, or helmets for riding our bikes. As children, we rode in cars with no seat belts or air bags. We drank water from the garden hose and not from prepared bottled water. We ate cupcakes, white bread, real butter, drank sodas but not overweight because we played outside most of the day, as long as we were home when the street lights came on. We spent hours building bicycles, scooters, soap box go-carts out of scraps then riding down the hill only to find out we forgot the brakes. After running into the bushes a few times, we figured out how to solve that problem. We fell out of trees, got cuts, broke bones with no lawsuits from the accidents. We played basketball with a real basket attached to the front of the shed.

To laugh is to rejoice in being alive.

You are wasting your time if you are holding anyone accountable for your happiness.

When we look back on our lives, how many of us are going to be pleased at how uptight we were.

Choose harmony, peace and love.

Max Lucado wrote a book called God will Carry You Through. Yes, God will and has carried me through especially since I viewed everything THROUGH BLESSED-TINTED GLASSES!